Published By Robert Corbin

VEGAN DIET

@ Chad Morris

Published By Robert Corbin

@ Chad Morris

Vegan Diet: Get Started With a Vegan Diet

All Right RESERVED

ISBN 978-87-94477-92-5

TABLE OF CONTENTS

Tempeh Salad 1

White Bean Salad 3

Butternut Squash 5

Faro And Veggies Split Pea Soup 7

Pumpkin Chili... 9

Tomato And Tofu Pizza... 11

Butternut Squash Risotto 13

Quinoa Falafel 14

Family Style Greek Salad 17

Zucchini Pasta... 20

Chocolate Peanut Butter Balls... 22

Chia Breakfast Pudding 24

Mixed Berry Smoothie Bowl.. 26

Blueberry Banana Muffins.. 28

Oatmeal Brown Bread 31

Zucchini Chocolate Bread 33

Chocolate Chip Pumpkin Muffins..................................... 36

Sweet Potato And Ginger Soup 38

Bean-Based Soups For Kidney Health Kidney Bean And Vegetable Soup 40

Lentil And Spinach Soup 42

Black Bean Burgers 44

Creamy Vegan Mushroom Risotto 49

Thai Green Curry 54

Quinoa And Chickpea Salad 59

Brown Rice And Black Bean Salad 60

Quinoa Salad 61

Classic Shout Ramen With Seared Tofu 62

Shout Ramen With Roasted Vegetable Medley 64

Spicy Shay Ramen With Sautéed Mushrooms 66

Baked Sweet Potato Chips 67

Quinoa Crispy Treats 69

Spinach Tofu Scramble 71

Chocolate Breakfast Quinoa 73

Banana Strawberry Oats 75

Rainbow Quinoa Salad 77

Rainbow Quinoa Salad 79

Creamy Tahini-Lemon Dressing...................................... 81

Lentil Soup.. 83

Tomato Soup 85

Vegan Chickpea And Avocado Wrap.............................. 87

Avocado And Zucchini Breakfast Bowl........................... 89

Chia Seed Pudding With Coconut Milk........................... 91

Keto Tofu Scramble 93

Instant Pot Ethiopian Lentil Stew 95

Rice And Beans 98

Perfect Instant Pot Brown Rice 102

Tuna Salad Sandwiches 104

Shine Salad 106

Mock Chicken Salad.. 108

Black Bean Lentil Salad... 110

Pumpkin Chick'n Chowder 113

Veggie Burger 116

Hawaiian Salad 119

Lentil Loaf With Tomato.. 121

Maple Flavored Oatmeal.. 125

Cinnamon Roll Muffins.. 127

Curried Tofu Scramble... 130

Sweet Potato Porridge Bowl 133

Almond Granola 135

Mushroom Bacon Over Toast 137

Zucchini Blueberry Muffins 141

Tempeh Salad

Ingredients:

- 2 green onions, diced
- 3 celery ribs, diced
- 3 tablespoons sweet relish
- 1 cup of your favorite vegan mayo
- 1 tablespoon spicy brown mustard
- 1 -8 oz package plain tempeh, crumbled
- 1/4 medium red onion, diced
- Sea salt and pepper to taste

Directions::

1. Crumble tempeh and mix with the red onion, green onion, celery, relish, mayo and brown mustard.

2. Add salt and pepper to taste.
3. Serve cold on salads or grilled in a sandwich.

White Bean Salad

Ingredients:

- 1/2 cup fresh basil leaves, torn into 1/2-inch pieces
- 1 tsp coarse sea salt or kosher salt
- Fresh ground black pepper
- 1/4 cup good quality olive oil
- 2 15.8-ounce cans Great Northern Beans, rinsed and drained
- 1/2 pound small Roma or plum tomatoes, chopped
- 3 cloves garlic, minced

Directions::

1. Combine beans, tomatoes, basil, and salt in a bowl, and season with pepper. Heat oil in a skillet over medium heat. Add garlic, and cook, stirring, until fragrant but not browned, just a minute or two.
2. Pour olive oil and garlic mixture over beans and tomatoes, and toss gently to combine.
3. Allow the bean salad to stand 30 minutes before serving to allow the flavors to meld.
4. Salad can be covered and kept at room temperature up to 4 hours.
5. Makes six servings of white bean salad.

Butternut Squash

Ingredients:

- 3 cups water

- 1 cup butternut squash purée

- 1 clove garlic, minced

- 1 can (14.5 oz/411g) diced tomatoes with chipotle (or plain with ½ teaspoon powdered chipotle)

- 1 teaspoon marjoram

- ½ teaspoon chili powder

- 1 tablespoon fresh cilantro, chopped

- 1 cup dried beans (anasazi, pinto, et.)

- Juice of ½ lime

- Salt to taste

- Ground hot pepper, optional to taste

Directions::

1. The night before: Combine the dried beans and water in the slow cooker and cook on low overnight, 8 9 hours.
2. In the morning: Add the butternut squash, garlic, tomatoes, marjoram, and chili powder. Cook on low for 8 10 hours.
3. Before serving: Taste and adjust seasonings. Add salt, hot pepper, and lime juice.
4. You can also make a quick mexi-pizza if you spread the frijoles on a tortilla thinly and top with some vegan chorizo and a few veggies. (Note: there is a fat-free, gluten-free, soy-free chorizo recipe in the book!)

Faro And Veggies Split Pea Soup

Ingredients:

- 8 cups water
- 3 bay leaves
- 2 cups chopped turnip or potato
- 2 teaspoon gram masala
- 2 teaspoons smoked paprika
- 1 package Tuscan Fields farro ai funghi (or 1 1/2 cups plain farro plus 2 veggie bouillon cubes)
- 1 cup split peas
- 1 teaspoon turmeric
- salt and pepper, to taste

Directions::

1. Add everything but the salt and pepper to your slow cooker and cook on low for 8 to 10 hours (or high for 3 to 4 hours).
2. Before serving add salt and pepper to taste. You can add 1 to 2 cups water to thin out the soup if it's too thick for you.

Pumpkin Chili

Ingredients:

- 1 28 oz. can diced stewed tomatoes
- 1- 15 oz. can kidney or black beans, drained & rinsed
- 1 12 oz. bottle of chili sauce
- 1-2 tablespoons chili powder
- 2 teaspoons pumpkin pie spice
- 1-1/2 teaspoons salt'
- bag of meat-free crumbles (such as Boca Ground Crumbles)
- 1 medium onion, chopped
- 1 cup canned pumpkin (or squash)

- 1 teaspoon pepper

Directions::

1. In a crock pot, combine all INGREDIENTS: and slow cook on low for 3-4 hours.
   On the stove in a soup pot, combine all INGREDIENTS: and bring to a boil. Reduce heat, cover and simmer and for 1 hour.
2. Serve with your favorite chili toppings!
3. If you like spicy chili, consider adding a touch of Chipotle peppers in adobo sauce or cayenne pepper.
4. You can substitute lentils, bulgur wheat, or more beans for the crumbles

Tomato And Tofu Pizza

Ingredients:

- 1 large heirloom tomato, seeded and chopped (about 10 ounces)
- 1/2 cup (2 ounces) shredded tofu cheese
- 3/4 cup (3 ounces) crumbled spicy tofu
- 1 (13.8-ounce) can refrigerated pizza crust dough
- Cooking spray
- 1 garlic clove, halved

Directions::

1. Prepare grill to medium heat.
2. Unroll dough onto a large baking sheet coated with cooking spray; pat dough into a 12 x 9-inch rectangle.

3. Lightly coat dough with cooking spray.
4. Place dough on grill rack coated with cooking spray; grill 1 minute or until lightly browned.
5. Turn crust over.
6. Rub with garlic; sprinkle with tomato and tofu cheeses.
7. Close grill lid; grill 3 minutes.
8. Serve immediately.

Butternut Squash Risotto

Ingredients:

- 1 cup water
- 1 (12-ounce) package frozen pureed butternut squash
- 1/4 teaspoon salt
- 1/4 teaspoon freshly ground black pepper
- tablespoons grated fresh Parmesan cheese
- Grated fresh Parmesan cheese (optional)
- 1 1/4 cups uncooked Arborio rice or other medium-grain rice
- 2 teaspoons olive oil
- 2 1/2 cups fat-free, less-sodium chicken broth

- Thyme sprigs (optional)

Directions::

1. Combine rice and oil in a 1 1/2-quart microwave-safe dish, stirring to coat.
2. Microwave, uncovered, at HIGH 3 minutes.
3. Add broth and 1 cup water to rice mixture; microwave, uncovered, at HIGH 9 minutes.
4. Stir well; microwave, uncovered, at HIGH 6 minutes.
5. Remove from microwave; let stand minutes or until all liquid is absorbed.
6. While risotto stands, heat squash in microwave at HIGH 2 minutes or until warm.
7. Add squash, salt, pepper, and cheese to risotto.
8. Stir well to combine. Garnish with additional cheese and thyme sprigs, if desired.

Quinoa Falafel

Ingredients:

- ⅓ cup cooked quinoa

- 2 tbsp. cilantro (fresh coriander)

- 1 tbsp. ground cumin

- ¼ tsp salt

- ¼ tsp pepper

- 2 vegan "eggs" (such as Ener-G Egg Replacer)

- 540 mL can chickpeas, rinsed & drained

- 2 vegetable oil

- 1 medium onion, finely chopped

- 1 clove garlic, minced

Directions::
1. Blend all dressing INGREDIENTS: in a food processor or blender.
2. Set aside.

3. Pulse the chickpeas in a food processor until no more whole chickpeas remain.
4. Heat 1 tbsp. vegetable oil in a frying pan on medium heat and fry the onions and garlic until soft.
5. Combine chickpeas, onion mixture, quinoa, cilantro, cumin, salt, pepper, and vegan "egg" mixture.
6. Form the mixture into 12 balls, and flatten them slightly.
7. Heat a couple tablespoons vegetable oil in a frying pan on medium heat.
8. Add the falafel patties and cook for about 3 minutes on each side, or until lightly browned.
9. Serve with dressing, either straight-up, or in pita bread with lettuce, tomato, etc.

Family Style Greek Salad

Ingredients:

Salad

- Chopped fresh parsley, ½ cup
- Chopped romaine lettuce, four cups
- Salt, ¼ teaspoon
- Diced yellow bell pepper, one
- Sliced black olives, ½ cup
- Sliced cherry tomatoes, one cup
- One cucumber peeled and cut into bite-sized chunks
- Nutritional yeast, ½ cup
- Olive oil, 2 tablespoons

Dressing

- Salt, ¼ teaspoon

- Minced garlic, 1 tablespoon

- Oregano, ¼ teaspoon

- Black pepper, ½ teaspoon

- Olive oil, 1/3 cup

Directions::

1. Place the dressing INGREDIENTS: in a large glass jar or a small bowl and mix them well. Put this off to the side to let the flavors blend while you make the salad.
2. Set out a large mixing bowl or salad serving bowl for the salad.
3. Place the chopped romaine lettuce into the bowl.

4. Drop in the chopped onion, diced bell pepper, sliced tomatoes and olives, and the chunks of cucumbers.
5. Use salad tongs or two large serving spoons to gently toss the salad INGREDIENTS: together until they are well blended.
6. Sprinkle the chopped fresh parsley over the top of the salad.
7. Divide the salad evenly among six serving bowls.
8. Drizzle the prepared salad dressing on the bowls of salad and then sprinkle on the nutritional yeast.

Zucchini Pasta

INGREDIENTS:

- Salt, ½ teaspoon

- Walnut if required

- Black pepper, 1 teaspoon

- Minced garlic, 3 tablespoons

- Olive oil, 4 tablespoons

- Nutritional yeast, ½ cup

- Ten Kalamata olives sliced in half

- Diced tomatoes, ½ cup

- Fresh zucchini, two large cleaned and cut into spirals

Directions::

1. Fry the zucchini in olive oil in a large skillet with salt and pepper for about ten minutes. Stir occasionally, and only cook until the zucchini spirals feel tender.
2. You can use 24 ounces of frozen zucchini zoodles if you prefer. Just let them thaw and then squeeze them gently with paper towels to remove the excess liquid.
3. Drain off the excess oil.
4. Stir in the garlic, sliced olives, and tomatoes.
5. Mix the INGREDIENTS: well and cook for five more minutes, stirring twice.
6. Pour the zoodle pasta into a serving bowl and sprinkle the nutritional yeast all over the top.

Chocolate Peanut Butter Balls

INGREDIENTS:

- Coconut flour, ¾ cup

- Agave nectar, ½ cup

- Smooth peanut butter, 2 cups

- Sugar-free chocolate chips, 2 cups

Directions::

1. Place parchment paper on a large plate or a tray and set it off to the side.
2. Put the peanut butter into a medium-sized mixing bowl.
3. Stir in the agave nectar and blend it well with the peanut butter.
4. Mix in the coconut flour, stirring until it all disappears. If this batter seems a bit dry and

crumbly, add a few drops of water until it is a smooth batter.

5   Make the batter into small balls with your hands, put them on the paper-lined tray, and then freeze them for 10 minutes.

6   While the batter balls are in the freezer, melt the chocolate chips in the microwave or a double boiler.

7   Pierce each ball individually with a fork, dip it into the melted chocolate and then place it back on the tray to let the chocolate harden.

8   Put them in the refrigerator for twenty minutes to let the chocolate become firm.

Chia Breakfast Pudding

Ingredients:

- ¼ teaspoon ground cinnamon
- 1 tablespoon unsalted roasted pistachios, chopped
- A pinch of ground cardamom
- A pinch of ground cloves
- 2 tablespoons chia seeds
- 2 teaspoons maple syrup
- ½ cup unsweetened almond milk
- ½ cup banana, sliced
- ¼ teaspoon vanilla extract

Directions::

1. Add chia seeds, maple syrup, almond milk, vanilla extract, cinnamon, cardamom, and cloves to a small bowl. Mix well.
2. Cover and refrigerate for at least 8 hours. This can be refrigerated for up to 3 days. Ideally, this is done overnight so that the pudding can be eaten for breakfast.
3. When it is time to serve, mix well. Divide the pudding mixture into 2 and place into 2 serving bowls. Top with the banana slices and chopped pistachios.

Mixed Berry Smoothie Bowl

Ingredients:

- ½ cup unsweetened almond milk
- ¼ cup pineapple chunks
- 1 teaspoon chia seeds
- ¼ cup kiwi, sliced
- 1 tablespoon toasted almonds, sliced
- 1 cup frozen mixed berries
- 1 large banana, peeled
- 1 tablespoon unsweetened coconut flakes

Directions::

1. Add the banana, mixed berries, and almond milk to a blender. Blend to a smooth consistency

2. Put the smoothie into a bowl and top with the pineapple chunks, kiwi slices, almond slices, coconut flakes, and chia seeds.
3. Serve immediately.

Blueberry Banana Muffins

Ingredients:

- ¾ cup of almond milk
- 1 teaspoon apple cider vinegar
- 2 cups oat flour
- 1 tablespoon cornstarch
- teaspoons baking powder
- ½ teaspoon salt
- 1 tablespoon flax meal
- 1 teaspoon vanilla extract
- 1 cup fresh blueberries, chopped
- 2 ripe bananas, mashed

- ⅓ cup maple syrup

- 2 teaspoon coconut oil, melted

- ⅓ cup coconut sugar

- ⅓ cup coconut flour

Directions::

1. Preheat your oven to 350 degrees F.
2. Prepare a muffin tin by lining it with 12 paper liners.
3. Combine the almond milk and apple cider vinegar in a small bowl. Set aside.
4. In a large bowl, combine almond flour, oat flour, cornstarch, baking powder, and salt. Whisk well to ensure the dry INGREDIENTS: are thoroughly combined.
5. Add the mashed bananas, maple syrup, coconut oil, vanilla extract, flax meal, and almond milk mixture to a medium bowl. Stir to combine.

6. Add wet mixture to dry INGREDIENTS: and stir to thoroughly combine. Fold in blueberries and coconut sugar.
7. Pour batter into prepared muffin tin. Bake for 20 minutes or until the top of the muffins are golden brown and firm.
8. Remove the muffins from the oven and allow to cool before serving. Can be stored in the refrigerator or at room temperature in an airtight container for up to 4 days.

Oatmeal Brown Bread

Ingredients:

- 2 teaspoons baking powder
- 1 1/2 teaspoons salt
- 1 teaspoon baking soda
- 1 1/2 cups soy milk
- Egg substitute (2 egg equivalents)
- 2 tablespoon olive oil
- 2-1/2 cups course whole wheat flour
- 1 cup oatmeal
- 3/4 cup wheat germ
- 2 teaspoons sugar

Directions::

1. In a medium bowl, mix all the dry INGREDIENTS: - flour, oatmeal, wheat germ, sugar, baking powder, salt, and baking soda. Create a well in the middle of the dry INGREDIENTS:.
2. In the well, add the milk, eggs, and olive oil; mix the batter well. If the mix is too thick, add a little more milk if necessary.
3. In a greased bread pan, add the batter and smooth the top. Make two diagonal cuts on the top of the bread.
4. Bake in the oven at 425 degrees F for 15 minutes. Reduce the heat to 375 F and bake for another 40 minutes.
5. Take out of the oven and test to see if done. To test if the bread is done, either tap the bottom and listen for a hollow sound or insert a skewer into the middle of the loaf and check if it comes out clean. If not, bake for another few minutes and re-check.

Zucchini Chocolate Bread

Ingredients:

- 1 tablespoon cinnamon
- 1 teaspoon baking soda
- 1/2 teaspoon baking powder
- 1 teaspoon salt
- 2 cups sugar
- 1 cup vegetable oil
- 2/3 cup soy milk
- 1 teaspoon vanilla
- 2 cups zucchini, shredded
- 2 tablespoons ground flax + 10 tablespoons water

- 1 cups flour

- 1/4 cup cocoa powder

- 1 cup vegan semi-sweet chocolate chips

- 1 cup walnuts, chopped, optional

Directions::

1. Preheat oven to 350 F. Spray two 9x5 inch loaf pans with nonstick spray.
2. For flax eggs, microwave flax meal and water for 30 seconds, stir, microwave, 30 more seconds, and stir again.
3. Combine all dry INGREDIENTS: in a large bowl and mix well. Add vegetable oil, and use a fork to stir. It will be dry but stir as well as possible.
4. Then add the flax eggs. Continue to mix.
5. Add milk and vanilla, and stir until well blended. Add zucchini, chocolate chips and walnuts, if using, and blend them in. The

mixture should be nice and smooth; moist looking.

6   Spoon into prepared loaf pans. Bake 55-60 minutes. Cool in pans for 10 minutes, then remove and cool completely.

Chocolate Chip Pumpkin Muffins

Ingredients:

- 3/4 cup canned pumpkin

- 1/4 cup water

- 1-1/2 cups flour

- 3/4 teaspoon baking powder

- 1/2 teaspoon baking soda

- 1/2 teaspoon ground cinnamon

- 1/4 teaspoon salt

- 3/4 cup sugar

- 1/4 cup canola oil

- Egg substitutes (2 egg equivalent), prepared

- 1/2 cup vegan chocolate chips

Directions::

1 Preheat the oven to 400 degrees F. Grease and flour muffin pan or use paper liners.
2 In a bowl, mix sugar, oil, and egg replacer. Add pumpkin and water.
3 In separate bowl, mix flour, baking powder, baking soda, cinnamon, and salt. Add the wet mixture and stir in chocolate chips.
4 Fill muffin cups 2/3 full with batter and bake for 20 to 25 minutes.

Sweet Potato And Ginger Soup

Ingredients:

- 1 onion, diced
- 2 tablespoons grated fresh ginger
- 1 cups low-sodium vegetable broth
- 2 large sweet potatoes, peeled and diced
- 1/2 cup unsweetened almond milk

Directions::

1. In a large pot, sauté the onion and grated ginger until they are soft and fragrant.
2. Add the diced sweet potatoes and low-sodium vegetable broth.
3. Bring to a boil and simmer for 20-25 minutes until the sweet potatoes are tender.
4. Puree the soup with an immersion blender until smooth.

5 Stir in almond milk and warm the soup without boiling. Serve.

Bean-Based Soups For Kidney Health Kidney Bean And Vegetable Soup

Ingredients:

- 2 cloves garlic, minced
- 2 cups low-sodium vegetable broth
- 1 cup diced tomatoes (canned or fresh)
- 1 teaspoon cumin
- 1 teaspoon paprika
- 1 cup kidney beans, soaked and cooked
- 1 onion, chopped
- 2 carrots, diced
- 2 celery stalks, chopped
- Salt substitute and pepper to taste

Directions::

1. In a large pot, sauté the onion, carrots, celery, and garlic until softened.
2. Add the kidney beans, vegetable broth, diced tomatoes, and spices.
3. Bring to a boil, then simmer for 30-40 minutes.
4. Season with salt substitute and pepper. Serve.

Lentil And Spinach Soup

Ingredients:

- 2 cloves garlic, minced
- 2 cups low-sodium vegetable broth
- 2 cups fresh spinach leaves
- 1 teaspoon cumin
- 1 teaspoon turmeric
- 1 cup green or brown lentils, rinsed
- 1 onion, chopped
- 2 carrots, diced
- 2 celery stalks, chopped
- Salt substitute and pepper to taste

Directions::

1. In a large pot, sauté the onion, carrots, celery, and garlic until softened.
2. Add the lentils, vegetable broth, and spices.
3. Bring to a boil, then simmer for 20-25 minutes.
4. Stir in the fresh spinach and cook for an additional 2-3 minutes until wilted.
5. Season with salt substitute and pepper. Serve.

Black Bean Burgers

Ingredients:

- 1/2 teaspoon smoked paprika

- 1 tablespoon soy sauce or tamari

- 2 tablespoons tomato paste

- 1/4 cup chopped fresh cilantro or parsley

- 1/4 cup breadcrumbs or oat flour (for gluten-free option)

- Salt and pepper to taste

- 1 can (15 oz) black beans, drained and rinsed

- 1/2 cup cooked quinoa or rolled oats

- 1/2 cup finely chopped onion

- 1/2 cup grated carrot

- 2 cloves garlic, minced

- 1 teaspoon ground cumin

- 1 teaspoon chili powder

- 2 tablespoons olive oil

Optional Toppings:

- Whole wheat or gluten-free burger buns

- Lettuce leaves

- Sliced tomatoes

- Sliced red onion

- Avocado slices

- Vegan cheese slices

- Ketchup, mustard, or your favorite burger sauce

Directions::

1. In a large mixing bowl, mash the black beans with a fork or potato masher until they are partially mashed but still have some texture.
2. Add the cooked quinoa or rolled oats, finely chopped onion, grated carrot, minced garlic, ground cumin, chili powder, smoked paprika, soy sauce (or tamari), and tomato paste to the bowl with the mashed black beans.
3. Mix all the INGREDIENTS: together until well combined. The mixture should be sticky enough to form patties. If it's too wet, add breadcrumbs or oat flour gradually until the desired consistency is reached. Season with salt and pepper to taste.
4. Divide the mixture into 4 equal portions and shape each portion into a round patty, about 1/2 to 3/4 inch thick.

5. Place the patties on a plate and refrigerate them for about 15-30 minutes to help them firm up.
6. In a large skillet, heat 1 tablespoon of olive oil over medium heat.
7. Add the black bean patties to the skillet and cook for about 4-5 minutes on each side, or until they are nicely browned and heated through. Add more oil if needed.
8. While the patties are cooking, you can toast the burger buns if desired.
9. Assemble your vegan black bean burgers by placing a cooked patty on the bottom half of each bun. Add your favorite toppings such as lettuce leaves, sliced tomatoes, sliced red onion, avocado slices, vegan cheese, and burger sauce.
10. Top with the other half of the burger buns and press down gently.

11. Serve these delicious vegan black bean burgers with a side of sweet potato fries, salad, or your favorite side dish for a satisfying and hearty meal!
12. Enjoy the plant-based goodness of these flavorful black bean burgers!

Creamy Vegan Mushroom Risotto

Ingredients:

- 2 cloves garlic, minced

- 1 oz (225g) cremini mushrooms, sliced

- 2 oz (225g) shiitake mushrooms, stems removed and sliced

- 1/4 cup dry white wine (optional)

- 1/2 cup unsweetened plant-based milk (such as almond or soy milk)

- 2 tablespoons nutritional yeast (optional, for added cheesy flavor)

- 1 tablespoon vegan butter

- Salt and pepper to taste

- 1 1/2 cups Arborio rice (or any medium-grain rice suitable for risotto)

- 2 cups vegetable broth

- 1 cup water

- 1 tablespoon olive oil

- 1 medium onion, finely chopped

- Fresh parsley or thyme for garnish (optional)

Directions::

1. In a medium saucepan, heat the vegetable broth and water. Bring it to a simmer and keep it warm over low heat.
2. In a large skillet or a wide saucepan, heat the olive oil over medium heat.
3. Add the finely chopped onion and sauté for about 2-3 minutes until it becomes translucent.

4. Stir in the minced garlic and cook for an additional 1-2 minutes until the garlic is fragrant.
5. Add the sliced cremini mushrooms and shiitake mushrooms to the skillet. Cook for about 5-7 minutes, or until the mushrooms are tender and slightly browned.
6. If using, pour in the dry white wine and cook for another minute to allow the alcohol to evaporate.
7. Stir in the Arborio rice and cook for about 1-2 minutes, making sure the rice is well coated with the oil and mushroom mixture.
8. Begin adding the warm vegetable broth and water mixture, one ladleful (about 1/2 cup) at a time, to the rice. Stir the rice constantly and allow the liquid to be absorbed before adding the next ladleful. Continue this process until the rice is creamy and cooked to your desired

level of tenderness. It should take about 20-25 minutes.

9. Once the rice is cooked and creamy, stir in the unsweetened plant-based milk and nutritional yeast (if using) to add creaminess and a hint of cheesiness.

10. Add vegan butter to the risotto and stir until it melts and incorporates into the rice.

11. Season the creamy mushroom risotto with salt and pepper to taste. Adjust the seasonings according to your preference.

12. Remove the skillet from heat and let the risotto rest for a minute or two before serving.

13. To serve, divide the creamy vegan mushroom risotto among individual plates or bowls.

14. Garnish with fresh parsley or thyme, if desired, for added flavor and presentation.

15. Enjoy this rich and indulgent creamy vegan mushroom risotto as a delightful main dish or

a side to complement your favorite plant-based meals!

Thai Green Curry

Ingredients:

For The Green Curry Paste:

- 1 tablespoon fresh basil leaves
- 1 tablespoon fresh lime juice
- 1 teaspoon ground coriander
- 1/2 teaspoon ground cumin
- 1/2 teaspoon ground turmeric
- 1/4 teaspoon white pepper
- 2 tablespoons vegetable broth or water
- 2 shallots, roughly chopped
- cloves garlic
- 1 stalk lemongrass, sliced (tender part only)

- 1 thumb-sized piece of ginger, sliced

- 1 green chili, seeded and chopped (adjust to your spice preference)

- 1 tablespoon fresh cilantro leaves

For The Green Curry:

- 1 cup broccoli florets

- 1 cup baby corn

- 2 tablespoons soy sauce or tamari

- 1 tablespoon agave syrup or brown sugar

- 1 tablespoon lime juice

- Fresh basil leaves and sliced red chili for garnish (optional)

- 1 tablespoon coconut oil or vegetable oil

- 1 can (14 oz) coconut milk
- 1 cup vegetable broth
- 1 cup sliced tofu or tempeh
- 1 cup sliced mixed vegetables (bell peppers, zucchini, carrots, etc.)
- Cooked jasmine rice or rice noodles for serving

Directions::

Green Curry Paste:

1. In a food processor or blender, combine all the green curry paste INGREDIENTS:: shallots, garlic, lemongrass, ginger, green chili, cilantro, basil, lime juice, ground coriander, ground cumin, ground turmeric, white pepper, and vegetable broth or water.
2. Blend the INGREDIENTS: until you get a smooth and well-combined paste. If needed,

you can add a little more water or broth to achieve the desired consistency. Set the green curry paste aside.

Green Curry:

3. In a large skillet or wok, heat coconut oil or vegetable oil over medium heat.
4. Add the green curry paste to the skillet and cook for 1-2 minutes, stirring constantly to release its aroma.
5. Pour in the coconut milk and vegetable broth, stirring well to combine with the green curry paste.
6. Add the sliced tofu or tempeh to the curry sauce and let it simmer for a few minutes to absorb the flavors.
7. Stir in the mixed vegetables, broccoli florets, and baby corn. Cook until the vegetables are tender-crisp.
8. Season the green curry with soy sauce (or tamari), agave syrup (or brown sugar), and

lime juice. Adjust the seasoning according to your taste preferences.

9 Once the vegetables are cooked to your liking, remove the green curry from heat.

Quinoa And Chickpea Salad

Ingredients:

- Cherry tomatoes, halved
- Cucumber, diced
- Red onion, finely chopped
- Fresh parsley, chopped
- Cooked quinoa
- Chickpeas, cooked
- Lemon vinaigrette

Directions::

1 Combine quinoa, chickpeas, cherry tomatoes, cucumber, red onion, and fresh parsley. Toss with a lemon vinaigrette.

Brown Rice And Black Bean Salad

Ingredients:

- Corn kernels

- Avocado, diced

- Red bell pepper, diced

- Cilantro, chopped

- Cooked brown rice

- Black beans, drained and rinsed

- Lime dressing

Directions::

1. Mix brown rice, black beans, corn, avocado, red bell pepper, and cilantro. Drizzle with a lime dressing.

Quinoa Salad

Ingredients:

- Cherry tomatoes, halved
- Cucumber, diced
- Red onion, thinly sliced
- Feta cheese (optional)
- Cooked quinoa
- Kalamata olives, sliced
- Greek dressing

Directions::

1 Combine quinoa, olives, cherry tomatoes, cucumber, red onion, and feta cheese. Toss with a Greek dressing.

Classic Shout Ramen With Seared Tofu

Ingredients:

- 2 tbsp mirin
- 1 tbsp sake
- 1 tbsp sugar
- 1 cup spinach, chopped
- 1 green onions, sliced
- 2 oz ramen noodles
- 2 tbsp sesame oil
- 1 block firm tofu, sliced
- 1 cups vegetable broth
- 1/4 cup soy sauce

- Nori sheets for garnish

Directions::

1 Cook ramen noodles according to package Directions::. Drain and set aside.
2 Heat sesame oil in a pan over medium heat. Sear tofu slices until golden brown on both sides.
3 In a separate pot, combine vegetable broth, soy sauce, mirin, sake, and sugar. Bring to a simmer.
4 Add cooked ramen noodles to the broth. Stir in spinach until wilted.
5 Divide ramen into bowls. Top with seared tofu, green onions, and nori sheets.

Shout Ramen With Roasted Vegetable Medley

Ingredients:

- 1 cup snap peas, halved
- 2 cups vegetable broth
- 1/3 cup soy sauce
- 1 tbsp sesame oil
- 1 tbsp rice vinegar
- 1 tbsp ginger, minced
- cloves garlic, minced
- 1 tsp chili flakes (optional)
- 2 oz ramen noodles
- 1 cups broccoli florets

- 1 bell pepper, sliced

- 1 carrot, julienned

- Green onions for garnish

Directions::

1. Preheat the oven to 400°F (200°C). Toss broccoli, bell pepper, carrot, and snap peas with sesame oil. Roast for 20-25 minutes.
2. In a pot, combine vegetable broth, soy sauce, rice vinegar, ginger, garlic, and chili flakes. Simmer for 15 minutes.
3. Cook ramen noodles according to package Directions::. Drain.
4. Divide noodles into bowls, add roasted vegetables, and pour hot broth over them.
5. Garnish with green onions.

Spicy Shay Ramen With Sautéed Mushrooms

Ingredients:

- 1/4 cup soy sauce

- 1 tbsp sriracha (adjust to taste)

- 1 tbsp sesame oil

- 1 tbsp rice vinegar

- 1 tsp sugar

- 2 cups bok choy, chopped

- 1 oz ramen noodles

- 2 tbsp vegetable oil

- cups mushrooms (shiitake, oyster), sliced

- cups vegetable broth

- 1 boiled eggs, halved

Directions::

1. Cook ramen noodles according to package Directions::. Drain and set aside.
2. In a pan, sauté mushrooms in vegetable oil until golden brown.
3. In a pot, combine vegetable broth, soy sauce, sriracha, sesame oil, rice vinegar, and sugar. Bring to a simmer.
4. Add bok choy to the broth and cook until tender.
5. Divide noodles into bowls, ladle hot broth over them, and top with sautéed mushrooms and boiled eggs.

Baked Sweet Potato Chips

Ingredients:

- medium-sized sweet potatoes, thinly sliced 2 tablespoons olive oil

- Salt and pepper to taste

- Optional: Seasonings like paprika, garlic powder, or rosemary

Directions::

1 Preheat oven to 375°F (190°C) and line a baking sheet with parchment paper.
2 Wash and dry sweet potatoes. Using a mandoline slicer or a sharp knife, finely slice the sweet potatoes.
3 In a bowl, mix the sweet potato slices with olive oil, salt, pepper, and other preferred spices until equally coated.
4 Arrange the slices in a single layer on the prepared baking sheet.
5 Bake for 15-20 minutes until the edges are crisp and golden brown.
6 Allow the Baked Sweet Potato Chips to cool before serving for a healthy and tasty crunch.

Quinoa Crispy Treats

Ingredients:

- ¼ cup honey or maple syrup

- ½ teaspoon vanilla extract

- 1 cups cooked quinoa

- ½ cup almond butter or other nut/seed butter

- Optional: Dark chocolate chips, chopped almonds, dried fruits

Directions::

1. In a mixing bowl, add cooked quinoa, almond butter, honey/maple syrup, and vanilla extract. Mix until completely blended.
2. If desired, add chocolate chips, almonds, or dried fruits to the mixture.
3. Press the quinoa mixture firmly into a baking dish lined with parchment paper.

4. Refrigerate for 1-2 hours until set.
5. Cut the chilled mixture into squares or bars to produce healthful and crunchy Quinoa Treats.

Spinach Tofu Scramble

Ingredients:

- 2 tbsp. Olive Oil

- 1 tsp. Lemon Juice, freshly squeezed

- ½ tsp. Soy Sauce

- Garlic cloves, minced

- Salt & Pepper, as needed

- 1 lb. Tofu, extra-firm & crumbled

- Tomatoes, finely chopped

- ¾ cup Mushrooms, finely sliced

- ½ red bell pepper, finely chopped

- 1 oz. Spinach

- 1 avocado (optional)

Directions::

1. First, take a medium-sized skillet and heat it over a medium-high heat.
2. Once the skillet becomes hot, spoon in the oil.
3. Next, stir in the tomatoes, red bell pepper, mushrooms, and garlic.
4. Cook them for 2 to 3 minutes or until softened.
5. Now, lower the heat to medium-low and spoon in the spinach, lemon juice, tofu, and soy sauce.
6. Mix well and cook for a further 8 minutes while stirring occasionally.
7. Then, check the seasoning and add salt and pepper as needed. Serve it hot.

Chocolate Breakfast Quinoa

Ingredients:

- 1 ½ cup Soy Milk

- 1 ½ tbsp. Maple Syrup

- 2 tbsp. Peanut Butter

- ½ cup Quinoa

- 1 ½ tbsp. Cocoa

- Banana and strawberry slices (for topping)

Directions::

1. First, place the quinoa and soy milk into a medium-sized saucepan over a medium-low heat.
2. After that, cook it for 13 to 15 minutes while keeping it covered.

3. Once the quinoa is cooked, stir in the peanut butter, sweetener, and cocoa powder to it.
4. Finally, transfer to a serving bowl.

Banana Strawberry Oats

Ingredients:

- ½ Of 1 banana, mashed

- 1 cup water

- ½ cup strawberries, sliced

- Dash of sea salt

- 1 tbsp. Flax meal

- ½ cup oats

- 1 cup zucchini, shredded

- 1 tbsp. Almonds, sliced

- ½ tsp. Cinnamon

- ½ scoop of protein powder

Directions::

1. First, combine oats, salt, water, and zucchini in a large saucepan.
2. Cook the mixture over medium-high heat and cook for 8 to 10 minutes or until the liquid is absorbed.
3. Now, spoon in all the remaining INGREDIENTS: to the mixture and give everything a good stir.
4. Finally, transfer the mixture to a serving bowl and top it with almonds and berries.
5. Serve and enjoy.

Rainbow Quinoa Salad

Ingredients:

- 1 cup cucumber, diced
- 1 cup bell peppers (red, yellow, or orange), chopped
- ½ cup red onion, finely chopped
- ½ cup fresh parsley, chopped
- ¼ cup fresh lemon juice
- 1 tablespoons extra virgin olive oil
- 1 cup quinoa, cooked and cooled
- 1 cup cherry tomatoes, halved
- Salt and pepper to taste

- Optional: ½ cup toasted nuts or seeds for garnish

Directions::

1. In a large bowl, combine quinoa, cherry tomatoes, cucumber, bell peppers, red onion, and parsley.
2. In a small bowl, whisk together lemon juice, olive oil, salt, and pepper.
3. Pour the dressing over the salad and toss gently to combine.
4. Refrigerate for at least 30 minutes before serving to allow flavors to meld.
5. Garnish with toasted nuts or seeds if desired before serving.

Rainbow Quinoa Salad

Ingredients:

- 1 cup bell peppers (red, yellow, or orange), diced
- 1/2 cup red onion, finely chopped
- 1 cup canned chickpeas, rinsed and drained
- 1/4 cup fresh parsley, chopped
- 1/4 cup fresh mint leaves, chopped
- Juice of 1 lemon
- 1 tablespoons extra-virgin olive oil
- 1 cup quinoa, rinsed
- 1 cups water or vegetable broth
- 1 cup cherry tomatoes, halved

- 1 cup cucumber, diced

- Salt and pepper to taste

Directions::

1. In a medium saucepan, bring water or vegetable broth to a boil. Add quinoa, reduce heat to low, cover, and simmer for 15-20 minutes or until quinoa is cooked and liquid is absorbed. Fluff with a fork and let it cool.
2. In a large mixing bowl, combine the cooled quinoa, cherry tomatoes, cucumber, bell peppers, red onion, and chickpeas.
3. Add chopped parsley and mint to the bowl.
4. In a small bowl, whisk together lemon juice, olive oil, salt, and pepper to make the dressing.
5. Drizzle the dressing over the salad and gently toss until well combined.
6. Taste and adjust seasoning if needed. Serve chilled.

Creamy Tahini-Lemon Dressing

Ingredients:

- 1 tablespoons water
- 1 garlic clove, minced
- 1 tablespoon maple syrup or agave nectar
- 1/4 cup tahini
- Juice of 1 lemon
- Salt and pepper to taste

Directions::
1. In a small bowl, whisk together tahini, lemon juice, water, minced garlic, maple syrup or agave nectar, salt, and pepper until smooth.
2. Adjust the consistency by adding more water if you prefer a thinner dressing.

3. Taste and adjust seasoning according to your preference.

Lentil Soup

Ingredients:

- 2 cloves garlic, minced

- 2 cups vegetable broth

- 1/2 teaspoon ground cumin

- 1/2 teaspoon ground coriander

- Salt and pepper, to taste

- 1 cup dried green or brown lentils, rinsed

- 1 onion, chopped

- 2 carrots, chopped

- 2 stalks celery, chopped

- 1 tablespoons olive oil

Directions::

1. In a large pot, heat the olive oil over medium heat.
2. Add the chopped onion, chopped carrots, chopped celery, and minced garlic to the pot and sauté until the vegetables are tender.
3. Add the rinsed lentils, vegetable broth, ground cumin, ground coriander, salt, and pepper to the pot.
4. Bring the soup to a boil, then reduce the heat to low and let it simmer until the lentils are tender, about 30 minutes.
5. Using an immersion blender, puree the soup until smooth. Serve hot.

Tomato Soup

Ingredients:

- 2 cups vegetable broth
- 1/2 teaspoon dried basil
- 1/2 teaspoon dried oregano
- Salt and pepper, to taste
- 1 tablespoons olive oil
- 2 cans diced tomatoes
- 1 onion, chopped
- 1 cloves garlic, minced
- 1/4 cup unsweetened coconut milk

Directions::

1. In a large pot, heat the olive oil over medium heat.
2. Add the chopped onion and minced garlic and sauté until the onion is translucent.
3. Add the diced tomatoes, vegetable broth, dried basil, dried oregano, salt, and pepper to the pot.
4. Bring the soup to a boil, then reduce the heat to low and let it simmer for 20-30 minutes.
5. Using an immersion blender, puree the soup until smooth.
6. Stir in the unsweetened coconut milk and heat the soup through.
7. Serve hot. These vegan soup recipes are delicious, healthy, and perfect for warming up on a chilly day. You can also experiment with different herbs and spices to add extra flavor.

Vegan Chickpea And Avocado Wrap

Ingredients:

- 1/2 red pepper, diced

- 1 tablespoon lemon juice

- Salt and pepper, to taste

- 1 can chickpeas, drained and rinsed

- 1 avocado, mashed

- 1/2 red onion, diced

- 1 whole wheat tortillas

Directions::
1. In a mixing bowl, mash the chickpeas and avocado together with a fork.

2. Add the diced red onion, red pepper, lemon juice, salt, and pepper to the bowl and mix everything together.
3. Divide the mixture evenly among the tortillas and roll them up tightly.
4. Cut the wraps in half and serve.

Avocado And Zucchini Breakfast Bowl

Ingredients:

- 2 medium zucchini
- 3 eggs
- Salt and pepper to taste
- 1 ripe avocado
- Optional toppings: cherry tomatoes, feta cheese, fresh herbs

Directions::
1. Scoop the flesh into a basin after halving the avocado and removing the pit.
2. Slice the zucchini finely or spiralize it.
3. To soften the zucchini, sauté it in a pan for three to five minutes over medium heat.
4. After you've pushed the zucchini to one side of the pan, break the eggs into the other.

5. While the zucchini is cooking, scramble the eggs and combine them.
6. Taste and add salt and pepper as needed.
7. After you've mashed the eggs and zucchini, spoon them over the avocado.
8. You may top it with feta cheese, cherry tomatoes, and fresh herbs if you want.

Chia Seed Pudding With Coconut Milk

Ingredients:

- 1 cup of coconut milk
- 1-2 tbsp. Honey or maple syrup
- 1/2 tsp vanilla extract
- 1/4 cup of chia seeds
- Fresh fruit for topping (e.g., berries, sliced banana)

Directions::
1. Mix the chia seeds, coconut milk, maple syrup or honey, and vanilla essence in a bowl.
2. Combine all of the INGREDIENTS: by whisking them together.
3. The chia seeds will absorb the liquid and form a pudding-like consistency if refrigerated for

at least 4 hours or overnight, covered in the dish.
4. Give the mixture a good stir just before serving.
5. Serve with a garnish of fresh fruit.

Keto Tofu Scramble

Ingredients:

- 2 bell pepper, diced

- 2 cups of spinach or kale, chopped

- 3 clove of garlic, minced

- 1 tsp turmeric powder

- Salt and pepper to taste

- 3 block of extra-firm tofu crumbled

- 2 tbsp. olive oil

- 1/2 onion, diced

- Nutritional yeast

Directions::

1. In a skillet set over medium heat, warm the olive oil.
2. Incorporate chopped bell pepper and onion, and cook until tender.
3. Cook the chopped greens and minced garlic until the greens wilt.
4. Scatter the tofu crumbles over the pan.
5. To add color to the tofu, sprinkle some turmeric powder on top.
6. Taste and add salt and pepper as needed.
7. Feel free to stir in some nutritional yeast for an extra taste boost.
8. Tofu should be cooked until it reaches a consistency similar to scrambled eggs.

Instant Pot Ethiopian Lentil Stew

Ingredients:

- 1/2 teaspoon cumin powder

- teaspoons berbere spice (adjust to taste)

- Salt to taste (a little more than 1/2 teaspoon)

- 2 tablespoons tomato paste

- 3/4 cup red lentils (135 grams)

- 1 cups vegetable broth (divided)

- 25-30 baby spinach leaves

- 2 tablespoons oil (use oil of choice)

- 1 inch ginger (10 grams, chopped)

- large garlic cloves (7 grams, chopped)

- 1 medium red onion (120 grams, sliced)

- 2 stalks of green onion, chopped

- Cilantro or parsley to garnish

Directions::

1. Press the sauté button on your Instant Pot. Once it displays hot, add the oil and then the chopped ginger, garlic, red onion, and spring onion.
2. Cook the onion, ginger, and garlic for around 3 minutes until softened. Then add the cumin powder and berbere spice. Also, add the salt, mix well, and cook for a few seconds.
3. Add the tomato paste, red lentils, and stir for 30 seconds. Then add 1.5 cups of vegetable broth and close the lid.
4. Press the manual or pressure cook button and cook on high pressure for 6 minutes, with the pressure valve in the sealing position.

5. Quick-release the pressure and then press the sauté button.
6. Add the remaining 1/2 cup of vegetable broth if desired at this point. I added the remaining 1/2 cup. Stir in the spinach leaves. Let it simmer for 1 minute or until the spinach leaves have wilted.
7. Serve this Instant Pot Ethiopian Lentil Stew with injera (the Ethiopian flat-bread) or plain rice! Garnish it with cilantro or parsley.

Rice And Beans

Ingredients:

- 1/4 teaspoon dried oregano

- 1/4 teaspoon onion powder

- 1/4 teaspoon garlic powder

- 1 (15 ounce) can black beans, drained and rinsed

- 1 (15 ounce) can corn kernels, drained and rinsed

- 1 cup + 2 tablespoons vegetable broth

- 1 cup white rice (brown rice will need more cooking time)

- 1 cup salsa

- 2 tablespoons olive oil

- 1 yellow onion, diced

- red bell peppers, diced

- garlic cloves, minced

- 1 teaspoon chili powder

- 1/2 teaspoon ground cumin

- 1/4 teaspoon smoked paprika

Burrito Bowl

- Shredded lettuce

- Chopped tomatoes

- Avocado

- Other toppings, as desired

Directions::

1. Turn on the Instant Pot and hit Saute. Add the oil, and once warm, add the onion and bell pepper. Cook until the onion and peppers are just tender, about 3-4 minutes.
2. Stir in the garlic and ground seasonings. Stir for just 30 seconds, until fragrant.
3. Turn the Instant Pot off, and add the rest of the INGREDIENTS:: beans, corn, vegetable broth, and rice. Stir together. Add the salsa on top, but don't stir in.
4. Cover and turn the vent to sealing. Hit manual pressure to 7 minutes.
5. When the cooking time is complete, do a quick release of the pressure (turn the vent to open, be careful- I use a kitchen towel to press it and then back away for the steam to release!) Remove the lid and stir together.
6. Make the burrito bowls! Divide the salad INGREDIENTS: among 4 bowls and top with the rice mixture. I like a little lime juice on

these bowls, but extra salsa, extra dressing, or no dressing works!

Perfect Instant Pot Brown Rice

Ingredients:

- 2 cups brown rice

- ½ cups of water

Directions::

1. Add the rice and water to the Instant Pot.
2. Close and lock the lid of the Instant Pot. Press Manual and set the timer to 22 minutes (it will take the Instant Pot 8-10 minutes to come to full pressure).
3. Once the time is up, you may do a "Quick Release" by pressing "Cancel" and twisting the steam-release handle on the lid.
4. Alternatively, opt for the "10-Minute Natural Release" by letting the pressure cooker go into "Keep Warm" mode, allowing it to sit for 10 minutes, then twisting the steam release handle.

5. After pressure is completely released, carefully remove the lid.
6. Serve immediately. Leftover rice can be stored in the freezer for 1 month or in the fridge for a week.

Tuna Salad Sandwiches

Ingredients:

- 2 tablespoons nori seaweed flakes

- 1 cup vegan mayonnaise

- 1 teaspoon salt

- 1/2 teaspoon black pepper, ground

- 12 slices of bread, lightly toasted

- large, crisp lettuce leaves

- 30 ounces (2 cans) garbanzo beans, drained

- 1/4 cup red onion, peeled and finely

- 1/2 cup celery, finely chopped

- 1/4 teaspoon garlic, minced

- 1/4 cup dill pickle, finely chopped

- 12 fresh tomato slices

Directions::

1. In a large bowl, mash the garbanzo beans with a potato masher or the back of a fork.
2. Fold the onion, celery, garlic, pickle, nori, mayonnaise, salt, and black pepper into the garbanzo beans. Combine thoroughly.
3. Lightly toast the bread.
4. Spread the salad on one slice and stack with a lettuce leaf, two tomato slices, and another slice of bread.
5. Cut sandwiches in half and serve.

Shine Salad

Ingredients:

- 1 tablespoon white wine vinegar
- 1 teaspoon agave nectar
- 1/4 teaspoon salt
- 1 cup chopped tomatoes
- 1 cup chopped cucumbers
- 1 (15oz) can garbanzo beans, drained and rinsed
- 1 cups cooked quinoa*
- 2 tablespoons good extra virgin olive oil
- big handfuls mixed greens
- 1 tablespoon sunflower kernels

Directions::

1. Mix garbanzo beans, quinoa, olive oil, vinegar, agave nectar, and salt in a large bowl.
2. Stir in remaining INGREDIENTS: when ready to eat.
3. If preparing in advance, keep remaining INGREDIENTS: stored separately.
4. A sprinkle of crushed red pepper or freshly cracked black pepper is also good on this salad.
5. You can use whatever vegetables you have on hand or enjoy.

Mock Chicken Salad

Ingredients:

- ½ cup dried fruit (I used goji berries, but raisins, cranberries, or chopped dates would also work)

- ¼ cup coarsely chopped walnuts or pecans

- t curry powder

- ½ t salt

- ½ t ground black pepper

- 2 oz (2 packages) tempeh, diced into small cubes

- 1 crisp apple, diced (Fuji or Granny Smith work well)

- 1 ¼ cup vegan mayonnaise (I used Veganaise)

Directions::

1. Steam tempeh for 10 minutes in a steamer basket placed over a pot filled with 2 to 3 inches of water.
2. Set aside and allow to cool completely.
3. Combine mayonnaise, curry powder, salt, and black pepper in a large bowl.
4. Stir in tempeh, apple, dried fruit, and nuts.
5. Cover and refrigerate until ready to serve. You may want to add a bit more mayonnaise to moisten before serving

Black Bean Lentil Salad

Ingredients:

- Juice of 1 lime

- 2 Tbsp. olive oil

- 1 tsp. dijon mustard

- 1-2 cloves garlic, minced

- 1 tsp. cumin

- 1/2 tsp. oregano

- 1/8 tsp. salt

- 1 cup dry lentils (green or brown)

- 15 oz. can black beans, rinsed and drained

- 1 red bell pepper

- 1/2 small red onion

- 1-2 roma tomatoes

- Large bunch cilantro, stems removed

- Optional: green onion

Directions:

1. Cook lentils according to package Directions:, leaving firm not mushy. Drain.
2. While lentils are cooking, make the dressing: place all INGREDIENTS: in a small bowl and whisk to combine. Set aside.
3. Finely dice the bell pepper, onion, and tomatoes. Roughly chop the cilantro.
4. In a large bowl, place the black beans, bell pepper, onion, tomatoes, and lentils. Add the dressing and toss to combine. Add cilantro, and lightly toss.

5. Serve immediately or chill covered in the fridge for at least an hour to let the flavors combine.

Pumpkin Chick'n Chowder

Ingredients:

- 1 1/2 cup vegan chick'n, cubed package (Gardein, Soy Delight, Smart Strips Chick'n, etc.)

- sprigs fresh thyme or 1 teaspoon dried

- 1 bay leave

- 1 tablespoon vegan chick'n bouillon, like Better than Bouillon (or 2 tablespoons of the one from my book if you have it)

- cups water

- cayenne or chipotle powder to taste

- 1 cup unsweetened non-dairy milk (I used So Delicious it's the thickest and great for soups.)

- 1/2 cup pumpkin purée

- 1 medium potato, diced

- cloves garlic, minced

- 1 cup corn kernels (fresh or frozen)

- salt and pepper to taste (will vary greatly on the bouillon used)

Directions:

1. The night before: Cut up the veggies and chick'n. Thaw pumpkin purée if you have it frozen. Store together in one bowl in the fridge.
2. In the morning: Add everything except the non-dairy milk, and the extra salt or pepper. Cook on low for 6 to 8 (or on high for 3 to 4 hours).
3. Remove bay leaf and thyme stems (if you used fresh thyme). Then add the non-dairy

milk and sour cream. Make sure you thoroughly mix them in the soup. Then taste your soup, and add more salt, pepper, cayenne, or thyme if needed.

4. If you want a thicker soup you can take about 1/3 of the soup and purée it in a blender or food processor and then mix it into the rest of the soup.

Veggie Burger

Ingredients:

- 1 tsp. oregano spice

- 1 tsp. mustard spice

- 1 tbsp. olive oil

- 1/2 cup diced onion

- 1 garlic cloves, minced

- 2 tbsp. sunflower seeds

- 2 sweet potatoes, washed

- 1/2 cup quinoa (dry)

- 1 cups cooked kidney beans, or 1 can no salt kidney beans, drained

- 1/2 cup buckwheat flour

- 1 tsp. cumin spice

- 1 cups spinach, washed and chopped

Directions:

1. Remove, flip and bake on other side for additional 20 minutes.
2. Put in between brown rice bread circles (aka English muffins), and top it with roasted red peppers, avocado and lettuce.
3. These served really well alongside baked brocollini with fresh ground black pepper. Bake sweet potatoes for 50 minutes at 400 degrees.
4. Meanwhile, boil the quinoa in 1 cup filtered water until cooked and fluffy.
5. Pour half of the kidney beans into a bowl and mash until paste-like texture forms.
6. Add remaining beans and lightly mash to combine.

7. When the sweet potatoes are cooked and soft, mash (with skins on) until mushy but not creamy.
8. Place the mashed sweet potatoes in a large bowl.
9. Stir the olive oil, buckwheat flour, oregano, cumin and mustard spices into the mashed sweet potatoes until combined throughout.
10. Mix in onion, garlic, quinoa, sunflower seeds, kidney beans and chopped spinach.
11. Preheat oven to 375 degrees and line a baking tray with parchment paper.
12. Form mixture into about 8 balls on the parchment paper and gently flatten them into patties about 1/2 inch thick each.
13. Bake in oven for 20 minutes.

Hawaiian Salad

Ingredients:

- 2 cups frisee, finely chopped
- 2 cups baby lettuce mix or baby spinach (any fave leafy green will work)
- 1 cup chopped pineapple
- 1 cup chopped papaya
- 3/4 cup roasted/salted macadamia nuts
- handful of plantain chips
- fresh black pepper

Pineapple Tahini Dressing

- 1 1/2 Tbsp. tahini sauce
- 1 tsp. Grade B maple syrup

- 1 Tbsp. apple cider vinegar

- 2 Tbsp. pineapple juice

- Pepper

Directions:

1. Whisk together the dressing.
2. Set aside.
3. Prep your fruit by chopping up your papaya and pineapple.
4. Store the leftovers. Finely chop your frisee. Place in bowl. Add baby lettuce.
5. Toss lettuce gently with 1-2 Tbsp. of dressing.
6. Portion salad into two bowls.
7. Add pineapple and papaya on top of lettuce.
8. Add macadamia nuts.
9. Place plantain chips around edges of bowls.
10. Drizzle additional dressing on top and add fresh black pepper to taste.

Lentil Loaf With Tomato

Ingredients:

- 1/4 cup tomato paste (or ketchup if none)
- 1/2 cup breadcrumbs
- 1/2 cup chopped walnuts
- 1/4 cup fresh parsley or 2 tablespoons dried parsley
- 1 tsp thyme or 1/2 teaspoon dried thyme
- 2 tbsp. tamari or soy sauce
- 2 tbsp. ground flaxseed
- 1 cups uncooked lentils and 4 cups of cooked lentils
- 2 tbsp. olive oil

- 1 medium onion, chopped super-tiny (half cup or so)
- stalks celery, chopped super-tiny (half cup or so)
- chopped carrots super-tiny (half cup or so)
- cloves of garlic
- salt and pepper

Glaze:

- 1/2 cup ketchup
- 2 tbsp. brown sugar
- 2 tsp. vinegar

Directions:

1. If using uncooked lentils, boil 2 cups of them in 5 cups of water.
2. Leave them until they are soft.

3. Pre-heat the oven to 350 degrees.
4. Chop the onion, celery and carrot as tiny as possible.
5. In a skillet add olive oil to heat and add the vegetables with a good pinch of salt.
6. When they are already starting to brown, stir in the garlic.
7. Leave it for about 10 min.
8. They're ready when the garlic is cooked.
9. Add the lentils with the remaining INGREDIENTS: and cooked vegetables in a large bowl.
10. Add salt and pepper.
11. Put the mixture into a loaf pan prepared with a piece of parchment paper first.
12. It is better if the paper come out of the mold, it make it easier when transferring to a serving platter.
13. Press the mixture with a spoon and top it with the glaze.

14. I add, about half of it. (To prepare the glaze, just mix all INGREDIENTS: in a bowl.)
15. Put the lentil loaf in the oven for 30-45 min. until it is browned and feels firm.

Maple Flavored Oatmeal

Ingredients:

- Walnuts, ½ cup

- Powdered Stevia, ¼ teaspoon

- Chia seeds, 4 tablespoons

- Almond milk, ½ cup

- Unsweetened coconut flakes, ¼ cup

- Ground cinnamon, ½ teaspoon

- Maple flavoring, 1 teaspoon

- Pecans, ½ cup

- Unshelled sunflower seeds, 3 tablespoons

Directions:

1. Pulse the walnuts, pecans, and sunflower seeds in a food processor until they are crumbly.
2. Put the maple flavoring and the almond milk in a medium-sized saucepan over medium heat and warm it slightly.
3. Stir in the crumbled nuts with the cinnamon, coconut flakes, stevia powder, and chia seeds until well mixed.
4. Simmer this for 30 minutes while you stir it often, so the chia seeds don't stick to the bottom of the saucepan.
5. Garnish the cooked oatmeal with a few fresh berries or a sprinkle of cinnamon or nutmeg.

Cinnamon Roll Muffins

INGREDIENTS:

Muffins

- Almond flour, ½ cup

- Baking powder, 1 teaspoon

- Vanilla flavored protein powder, two scoops

- Unsweetened applesauce or pumpkin puree, ½ cup

- Nut butter of choice, ½ cup

- Coconut oil, ½ cup

Glaze

- Coconut milk, ¼ cup

- Lemon juice, 2 teaspoons

- Coconut oil, ¼ cup

Directions:

1. Heat the oven to 350 F.
2. Put paper cups in the cups of a twelve-muffin pan and set it off to the side.
3. In a large-sized mixing bowl, mix the cinnamon, almond flour, baking powder, and vanilla protein powder until they are well mixed.
4. Stir in the coconut oil, nut butter, and the pumpkin puree or applesauce and blend everything well.
5. Blend until you have a creamy, smooth batter.
6. Divide the batter evenly between the twelve paper cups.
7. Cook the muffins on the middle oven rack for 10 to 15 minutes.
8. Leave the warm muffins in the pan for 5 minutes to cool.

9. After 5 minutes, set the muffins in their papers out on a wire rack. The muffins will be cooled in about 30 minutes.
10. Mix the recipe for the glaze, spread it on the muffins, or drizzle it over the tops.
11. Let the glaze harden for 5 minutes, and then serve the muffins.

Curried Tofu Scramble

Ingredients:

Sauce

- Salt, ½ teaspoon
- Ground paprika, ¼ teaspoon
- Ground cumin, ¼ teaspoon
- Garlic powder, ¼ teaspoon
- Garam masala, ¼ teaspoon
- Ground turmeric, ¼ teaspoon
- Ground coriander, ¼ teaspoon
- Curry powder, ½ teaspoon

Scramble

- Olive oil, 1 tablespoon

- Firm tofu, one eight-ounce block

- Button mushrooms, sliced, ¾ cup

- Diced onion, ¼ cup

- Red bell pepper, 1 large cleaned and diced

- Chopped fresh spinach, three cups

Directions:

1. Thirty minutes before cooking, place the block of tofu in between several layers of dry paper towels, set a clean plate on top, then put three or four cans of fruit or veggies on top of the container. This process will press the excess liquid out of the tofu.
2. Heat the olive oil in a large skillet over medium heat and fry the onions for three minutes.

3. Stir in the chopped bell pepper and slices of mushroom and fry for ten minutes, stirring often.
4. Push all of the fried veggies to one side of the skillet.
5. Put the tofu in the empty place in the skillet and crumble it, then cook it for five minutes, stirring occasionally.
6. While the tofu is cooking, blend the spices.
7. Sprinkle the spices over the mixture in the skillet, and then blend everything.
8. Blend in the chopped spinach and cook for five more minutes.

Sweet Potato Porridge Bowl

Ingredients:

- 1 large sweet potato

- 1 small ripe banana, mashed

- 2 tablespoons pecans, chopped

- 1 tablespoons dried cranberries

- Cinnamon to taste

Directions:

2. Preheat your oven to 375 degrees F.
3. Wash and dry sweet potato. Poke holes around the entire surface of the sweet potato several times. Wrap sweet potato in aluminum foil and bake for an hour and 20 minutes or until a fork easily pierces through the entire sweet potato.

4. Cool for at least 5 minutes then peel and discard the skin.
5. Add the peeled potato to a medium bowl along with the ripe banana and cinnamon. Likely mash the mixture.
6. Top with dried cranberries and chopped pecans, and serve immediately. Can be stored overnight in the refrigerator and reheated for later consumption.

Almond Granola

Ingredients:

- ½ cup coconut sugar
- ¼ cup canola oil
- 1 teaspoon of salt
- 1 teaspoon vanilla extract
- 1 cup raw almonds
- 1 cups gluten-free oats
- ½ cup sunflower seeds

Directions:
1. Preheat your oven to 350 degrees F.
2. Prepare 2 baking sheets by lining them with parchment paper.

3. In a large bowl, combine coconut sugar, canola oil, vanilla extract, and salt.
4. Add the rest of the INGREDIENTS: to the bowl and toss to ensure that the almonds and oats are coated well. Divide the granola mixture between the two prepared baking sheets. Spread out into even, thin layers on the baking sheets.
5. Bake for 20 minutes or until the mixture is golden brown on the top and crisp.
6. Remove from the oven and let cool completely before serving with fresh fruit, with dairy-free milk such as almond milk, over vegan ice cream or as a snack.
7. Can be stored at room temperature in an airtight container for up to 2 weeks.

Mushroom Bacon Over Toast

INGREDIENTS:

For Mushroom Bacon

- ⅛ teaspoon onion powder
- ½ teaspoon paprika
- Salt and pepper to taste
- Olive oil to drizzle
- 1 ½ cup dried mushrooms, finely chopped
- 1 teaspoon maple syrup
- ⅛ teaspoon garlic powder

For Toast

- ½ cup fresh parsley chopped
- Salt and pepper to taste

- Olive oil to drizzle

- slices almond bread (or any other gluten-free, dairy-free bread preferred)

- ½ cup chickpeas hummus (see recipe Chapter 5: Sauce and Condiment Recipes: Chickpea Hummus)

- 18 cherry tomatoes

Directions:
1. To prepare mushroom bacon, preheat your oven to 375 degrees F.
2. Prepare a baking sheet by lining it with parchment paper.
3. Place the finely chopped mushroom pieces on the baking sheet in a single layer. Drizzle with olive oil and season with salt and pepper.
4. Bake for 15 minutes. Remove from the oven and carefully toss mushrooms over. Return to

oven to bake for 15 more minutes or until the mushrooms are browned and crispy.

5. Remove the mushroom pieces from the oven and place in a large bowl. Blot with a paper towel to remove the excess oil.
6. Toss with maple syrup, garlic powder, onion powder and paprika. Return to the baking sheet and bake for 5 more minutes to caramelize the mushrooms.
7. Remove from the oven and set aside.
8. To arrange the toast, prepare 2 more baking sheets with parchment paper. Place the bread pieces on one and tomatoes on the other.
9. Place this on the bottom and top racks of the oven for the last 10 minutes that the mushroom pieces of bacon are baking. Remove when the slices of toast are golden brown and the tomatoes blister and soften.
10. Spread the desired amount of hummus on each piece of toast. Add the blistered

tomatoes, mushroom bacon bits, parsley, salt, and pepper. Drizzle with olive oil and serve.

Zucchini Blueberry Muffins

Ingredients:

- 1 teaspoon of vanilla extract

- 1/2 of a banana, mashed

- 3/4 of a cup of pureed zucchini

- 1/4 of a cup of unsweetened applesauce

- 1 cup of fresh blueberries

- 1 3/4 cups of flour

- 2 teaspoons of baking powder

- 1/2 of a teaspoon of allspice

- 1/4 of a teaspoon of salt

- 1/3 of a cup of sugar

- 1 tablespoon of water

Directions:

1. Combine dry and wet INGREDIENTS: separately. Mix them together, and fold in the blueberries.
2. Spoon into a muffin pan sprayed with cooking spray and bake at 400 F for 15 minutes.

www.ingramcontent.com/pod-product-compliance
Lightning Source LLC
LaVergne TN
LVHW010224070526
838199LV00062B/4722